Copyright 2014 by
Karla Oceanak and Allie Ogg

Published by:
Bailiwick Press
309 East Mulberry Street
Fort Collins, Colorado 80524
www.bailiwickpress.com

Book design by:
Launie Parry
Red Letter Creative
www.red-letter-creative.com

ISBN 978-1-934649-50-3

Library of Congress
Control Number:
2014939842

Printed in Canada

22 21 20 19 18

10 9 8 7

GOODNIGHT BREW

A Parody for Beer People

By Ann E. Briated

Illustrated by Allie Ogg

BAILIWICK PRESS

In the great brew room,
there was a kettle that shone,
and a gramophone,
and a pitcher of...

...a chocolate stout with two feathers of foam.

And there were three little otters in charge of the water.

For fermenting, some yeast.

And a hops wildebeest.

And a black bear named Charlie and sweet malted barley.

And bottles and clogs and a whirling wort hog.

And a flavorful cache
and a whole tun of mash.

And a baritone brewer with a foamy mustache.

Goodnight brew.

Goodnight crew.

Goodnight moony cockatoo.

Goodnight cache

and goodnight mash.

Goodnight kettle and tanks of metal.

Goodnight barley. Goodnight Charlie.

Goodnight wildebeest

and yeast.

Goodnight bottles and bear-foot waddles.

Goodnight saison.
Goodnight wheat.

Goodnight porter and clogg-ed feet.

Goodnight stout and IPA. Goodnight bock and hog ballet.

Goodnight waltz

and derrières.

Goodnight beer lovers everywhere.

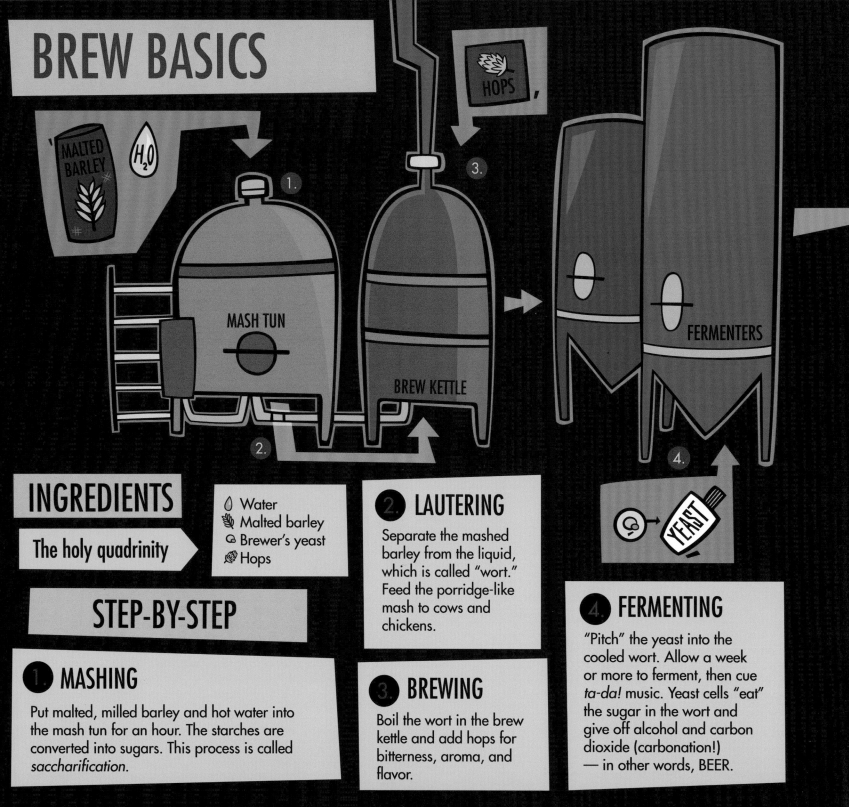

BREW BASICS

MALTED BARLEY

H₂O

HOPS

1. MASH TUN

3. BREW KETTLE

4. FERMENTERS

2.

YEAST

INGREDIENTS

The holy quadrinity

- 💧 Water
- 🌿 Malted barley
- 🍥 Brewer's yeast
- 🌿 Hops

STEP-BY-STEP

1 MASHING

Put malted, milled barley and hot water into the mash tun for an hour. The starches are converted into sugars. This process is called *saccharification*.

2 LAUTERING

Separate the mashed barley from the liquid, which is called "wort." Feed the porridge-like mash to cows and chickens.

3 BREWING

Boil the wort in the brew kettle and add hops for bitterness, aroma, and flavor.

4 FERMENTING

"Pitch" the yeast into the cooled wort. Allow a week or more to ferment, then cue *ta-da!* music. Yeast cells "eat" the sugar in the wort and give off alcohol and carbon dioxide (carbonation!) — in other words, BEER.

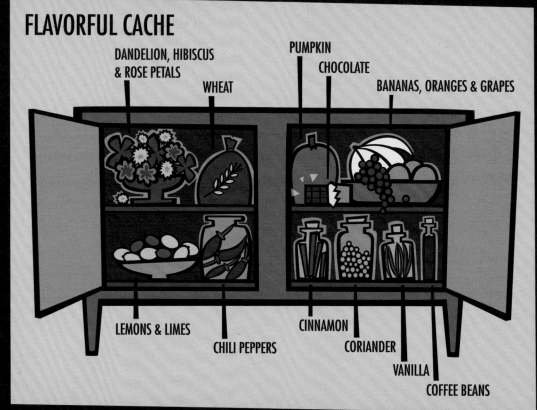

CONDITIONING TANK

5.

6.

FLAVORS

7.

Besides wort and hops, brewers can add lots of other goodies to the brew kettle to flavor the beer. The "flavorful cache" in this story shows a few "flavorites." Sometimes wheat, oats, or rye are added to malted barley in the mash.

5. CONDITIONING

After fermenting, beer spends time in a conditioning tank to allow its flavors to mature. Some beers are also filtered after conditioning and before being placed in ready-to-drink-from containers.

6. PACKAGING

Put the beer in the containers of your choice — kegs, bottles, cans, growlers, etc.

FLAVORFUL CACHE

DANDELION, HIBISCUS & ROSE PETALS

WHEAT

PUMPKIN

CHOCOLATE

BANANAS, ORANGES & GRAPES

LEMONS & LIMES

CHILI PEPPERS

CINNAMON

CORIANDER

VANILLA

COFFEE BEANS

7. DRINKING
Cheers!

BEER TYPES & STYLES

There are two main types of beer:

ALES & LAGERS

Ales have been around for thousands of years and are made from a yeast called *saccharomyces cerevisiae*, which ferments at warmer temperatures at the top of the brew. Ales tend to be fruity and aromatic, with a more robust, complex flavor, sometimes including bitter or sour.

The whippersnappers of the beer family tree, lagers have only been around for about 200 years. They are made from a yeast called *saccharomyces carlsbergensis*, which ferments at cooler temperatures at the bottom of the brew. Lagers tend to have a light, clean, crisp taste.

COMMON ALES

BLONDE   BROWN   IPA

PORTER   SAISON   STOUT   WHEAT

COMMON LAGERS

BOCK   DORTMUNDER   DUNKEL

OKTOBERFEST   PILSNER